# FOLLOW TO UNFOLLOW

# FOLLOW TO UNFOLLOW

## A GUIDE BOOK ON HOW TO BUILD REAL INSTAGRAM FOLLOWERS

### CARLOS A. SALGUERO
@CARLITOSKYISTHELIMIT

Charleston, SC
www.PalmettoPublishing.com

Follow to Unfollow

First Edition

Hardcover ISBN: 979-8-8229-0688-4

Paperback ISBN: 979-8-8229-0687-7

eBook ISBN: 979-8-8229-0686-0

# CONTENTS

# INTRODUCTION

**I AM WRITING THIS** book because a couple of years ago, I realized how powerful Instagram has become. Two of the things I love most about Instagram are that you can have unlimited followers and you can get paid to use it. Even though I really love thinking about numbers, I neglected Instagram for many years. I really thought that Instagram was not the best social media platform, but then I realized how powerful it can be.

I have loved and enjoyed Facebook for a very long time, and I still do. But unfortunately, Facebook accounts have a cap of five thousand followers—which really sucks. I am really trying to build my social media platform to thousands and thousands of real followers, and Instagram, unlike Facebook, can definitely help me—and many others—get there. As an entrepreneur, I need to build a strong social network to help me with my businesses. And what I've learned can help you too.

I've developed a method called "Follow to Unfollow," and this has definitely helped me increase my follower numbers dramatically. I started to use Instagram more than three years ago, and I have become very successful building up real followers using this method. Currently, I have more than thirty thousand real followers and more than one hundred certified followers. My short-term goal is to get over forty thousand followers by 2023 and my long-term goal is to have more than one hundred thousand real followers and about one thousand certified followers. Through trial and error, I've done well, but it took me more than three years to really understand the best way to attract real and certified followers. This book will give you ways to build your Instagram with real and certified followers and also to be aware of scammers.

# CHAPTER 1

# What Are Real Instagram Followers?

**TO UNDERSTAND WHAT REAL** Instagram followers are, we need to understand what fake followers are. When I first started to use Instagram, I had no idea what fake followers were. I didn't realize that you can download an external app to help you increase your Instagram followers. There are also different businesses that can help you buy and increase your followers. I can see why people would use this type of app or business to look cool, help their business get started, or become Instagram influencers.

I remember the first time that I found out about fake followers. My ex-girlfriend used Instagram all the time, and she had more than twenty thousand followers. I was very intrigued, so I asked her how she'd gotten so many followers. She took her phone out and showed me how to get fake followers on Instagram, which truly opened my eyes. Fake Instagram followers are usually bots or inactive accounts on Instagram that are created to follow other profiles and to boost their follower numbers. The fake profiles don't belong to real people, so they won't engage with your posts, but they make it seem like a profile has a lot of influence.

Don't waste your time buying followers or using any app that will give you fake followers. I used to visit certain profiles, see thousands and thousands of followers, and tell myself how cool that person was for having so many followers. But after I realized that those profiles mostly had fake followers, I didn't envy them anymore. I've never liked fake things in my life, especially fake followers, so I never used those types of apps or businesses to help me grow my followers.

The real question now is how to know whether a profile has fake followers. It's very simple: you must look at the person's pictures and videos to see how many likes and views they have. For example, if a profile has twenty thousand followers but its pictures have only twenty to one hundred likes, the profile most likely has fake followers. The same goes for views. If the same person with twenty thousand Instagram followers has only twenty to one hundred views on their videos, the person has fake followers. If you do the math, how can a person with so many Instagram followers have so few likes and views? A person with twenty thousand followers should have more than three hundred likes and one thousand views, easily.

So what are real followers? On Instagram, a real follower is a real person who follows your account and can see, like, and comment on your posts.

Yes, having thousands of followers is intriguing, but if your likes and views don't match your followers, it's not so intriguing anymore. Anyone can download an app or buy fake followers.

I personally believe that Instagram is all about real followers, real likes, and real views. This way, your account looks legit, and people who visit it know that your followers are real.

# CHAPTER 2

# What Is Follow to Unfollow?

**I AM SURE I'M** not the only person who does what I call Follow to Unfollow. It is a very simple system: I follow as many people as possible, they follow me back, and later I just unfollow them, hoping that the majority of my followers keep following me.

But you need to work the system. Growing your real Instagram followers means taking your time and being smart about who you follow. The main goal is to try to keep as many real followers as possible. Treat it like a game. The analogy I like to use is catching Pokémon. If you've never played Pokémon, basically, it's all about trying to catch Pokémon (like you're trying to catch real followers) and keep them.

When you start the unfollow process, first you need to know whether the profiles you've followed are following you back or not. To find out whether a person is following or not following you, go to their profile and click on their Following button. It will show you whether they are following you. If they are not following you back, always hit three Likes on their recent pictures, and then unfollow them. I never did this before because all I used to do was hit Unfollow at the beginning of my process, right after following someone. But when I started to like their pictures first, it made a huge difference in getting more followers. I don't mind when people don't follow me back; it gives me a chance to get more followers when I start my system, Follow to Unfollow.

As you unfollow people, you're going to start noticing which groups don't follow you the most, and you can go from there.

I've been using this system for more than three years, and I have increased my follower numbers to more than thirty thousand real followers. This system really works, but you must be smart about which followers you target. Always remember that the purpose of this system is just to follow to unfollow. Do not harass anyone; it's not a dating site. Stay focused because it's all about growing your followers.

# CHAPTER 3

## How to Build Your Instagram Numbers

**ONE THING I DID** find out through this process is not to add people who have a high followers base. The majority of times they just don't add anyone back. What does this mean? When you look at their profile, check how many people they have as followers. If those numbers are very high, keep moving to the next potential person you want to add. Let's talk about who are the best people to add. You only want to add people who have a high following base, as they will add mostly everyone back. This has definitely worked for me. Always remember the purpose is to add as many people as possible because in the long run you will unfollow them.

In the beginning of my process, I mostly used to follow people in the United States. I was very successful in getting them to follow me back and still am, but I came to realize that many of them do care about followers, especially the younger generation, those between the ages of eighteen and thirty. I found out that they don't follow back, and they want as many followers as possible too. Some will follow you and later unfollow you. Now I target Instagrammers from other countries, and most of my followers come from Venezuela. I also try to follow older adults because many will follow me back. They don't really care whether you unfollow them in the end, which is exactly what we want.

And make sure that you follow people who have private pages. It is much easier to get them to follow you back, in my personal experience; the ones who have public pages don't usually follow you back. But if you want to get public pages to follow you, you can do what I do, which is hit Like on three of their recent photos without following them. Many times, they want to know who you are and will hit Follow to see who liked their pictures. Try it because it will work at times. Sometimes, I like to put an emoji on just one of their pictures. I usually use a thumbs-up emoji, a birthday emoji if it is a birthday picture, or a prayer or heart emoji if it is something sentimental. You need to make sure that the emoji goes with the picture; this way, you have their attention. Not many people comment on pictures, so when you do, some will try to follow you out of curiosity. And if Instagrammers have only one to three pictures on their profile, definitely hit Like, and comment with an appropriate emoji. Some will even send you a follow request and will hit Like on some of your Instagram pictures; this way, you can get more views and likes on pictures.

Another way to get your views up is by paying Instagram directly, and they will expose your video or picture to hundreds or thousands of Instagrammers around your area or even further. But your profile account cannot be private; it has to be public for everyone to see. I have done it once, and it definitely has worked for me—I was able to get over sixteen thousand views on my video. It's really not too expensive; it all depends how long you want to market your picture or video. You have a choice from a few days to a month. The longer you want to market your picture or video, the more expensive it becomes. Try it once and see the difference in views and likes. In my personal opinion, I would rather market videos because of the views one receives. But once you are done, make sure to put your profile account back to private because a private account will get you more people to follow you back.

I am Latino, and the majority of the people I like to follow are from Spanish-speaking countries. Speaking Spanish helps me connect with them and helps me catch their attention. I have all different types of ethnicities, cultures, and nationalities featured on my Instagram, but it's easier to connect with my own culture, in my opinion. I also never prejudge anyone, because a follower is always great to have, no matter their nationality, ethnicity, or culture.

Let's talk about getting people's attention and catching their eye with your Instagram account. Two of the most important things you must have are a great profile picture and bio information. You need to make sure your profile picture is super nice. If you have a professional picture of yourself, definitely use that, but the picture must be eye-catching. Your bio information must also have great information—for example, you can include your education, your business if you have one, where you live, or even a positive quote. If you are American, put an American flag there, because many people from other countries love America and wish they were here; it's a great way for them to know someone who's American. As mentioned, I target Instagrammers from Latin countries, especially Venezuela. In my opinion, they do most of the following, and if I can get one million followers from Venezuela, I will. Now, you may be saying to yourself, "I don't know anyone from Venezuela." Don't worry; all you have to do is go to my profile, follow me, and look at all my followers. Once you find one, you will find them all. And once people notice how huge your follower numbers are, they are going to start following you. Big numbers mean success in their eyes.

Let's talk about which gender to follow. This is up to you. I prefer following women; the majority of women, but not men, will follow me back. I also feel more comfortable following women. When a man is trying to follow another man, he might get a little suspicious; the majority of men who don't know me won't follow me back. I've had many men follow me, but I do not follow them back, especially if I don't know them. In the beginning of my process, I tried to follow men, but the numbers who followed me back were very low. Remember, it took me more than three years, with trial and error, to understand who would follow me back.

Women who want to try this could have an advantage because they can follow both genders and it doesn't look too bad. Following men also comes with negatives because I'm sure that women will get a lot of messages in their inbox that could be very annoying. Some men may even send explicit pictures or videos that may not be appropriate. It's hard to really say because I'm not a woman, but I know that there are many perverts out there, and they might get the wrong impression. So it is up to you; just know it could lead to all this.

The best time to add people is in the mornings, in my experience. On a good day, I've gotten back seventy-five followers in one day. While there is research out there about the best time to be active on Instagram, from my personal experience, Wednesday, Thursday, and Friday mornings are the best times to start following Instagrammers. On weekends, my follower numbers have not been so great, so I try not to work my system then. I keep it only to the weekdays.

Another great way to build your Instagram numbers is linking your account to other social media. I don't know whether you know this, but Instagram is owned by Facebook/Meta, which is owned by Mark Zuckerberg. By linking your Instagram with other social media platforms, it will help with exposure, and this is a great way for you to get more followers.

When I start following Instagrammers, I follow a pattern of checking their most recent pictures and likes. For example, if they posted a picture the same day, a few days ago, or even a week before, I go through their likes to see who enjoyed it. I start following mostly everyone who hit Like. I do this because these Instagrammers are active and enjoy using Instagram. As I go through their likes and see open accounts, I start looking to see whether their pictures are recent, and so on and so forth. This is a pattern I followed when I started working on my system. The more you do it, the better you will get at it, similar to anything else. By the way, use the same concept once you start to unfollow people: check out their recent likes, and start working the system.

# CHAPTER 4

## Different Ways to Lose Followers

**THERE ARE SO MANY** ways you can lose Instagram followers. That is something I try to avoid because the goal of this system is to keep as many followers as possible, so this chapter is very important.

If your profile picture and your bio information are not eye-catching, you might lose followers. Posting too many pictures or videos in a day is another way to lose followers; no one really likes when Instagrammers spam their newsfeed. You must be very selective about what you post because one bad picture or post will get you unfollowed. Posting negative content is another way to lose followers because not many people like negative posts. It is better to post pictures and videos on your story rather than on your profile; many people don't mind looking at stories, but don't overdo it, especially if you do it every day.

Keep your page private rather than public; this way, Instagrammers feel special that they follow your private page. If your page is public, in my opinion, it is easy to know who you are, and there is no curiosity anymore. Following thousands and thousands of people is not attractive to Instagrammers; it shows that you're willing to follow just anyone, and many Instagrammers don't like that either, especially if you have a low follower count. If you're just starting, it's OK to follow as many people as possible, but once you're close to following four thousand, start to use the system Follow to Unfollow. This way, you have more followers than people following you. Little by little, you will see your Instagram followers go up, and you won't lose too many followers. That is exactly what our goal is. It's all a numbers game: work the system, and you will see a huge difference in numbers. But you need to do it right and be very patient. You will get there. Trust the process; it has worked very well for me.

Understanding all of this, I made a conscious decision to hardly post anything at all. I post only one picture or video a year, on my birthday. When I do, I lose about three hundred followers, which I know is going to happen. So knowing this, I don't post anything else. But that is OK because I still gain about five to seven thousand followers a year. If I want to post anything, it goes on my Facebook because my Instagram is only to build numbers. My goal is to get paid by sponsors once I reach more than fifty thousand followers.

I am building high numbers; this way, when people look at my Instagram, it's eye-catching, and the majority will not unfollow me. People love to get followed by Instagrammers with a huge following, but they don't know that later on, I will unfollow them. Many don't mind because they feel I must be someone popular and want to continue to follow my page. It's all a perception I try to use and will use for a very long time. Once I get the numbers I really want, I will start posting. But for now I am holding back because the goal is to really reach high numbers so that one day I can get paid.

# CHAPTER 5

## Can Instagram Help You Make Extra Income?

**LIKE I MENTIONED BEFORE,** I am trying to get so many followers because one day I would love to get paid by sponsors and make extra income. There are so many people making a lot of money on Instagram, and if they can do it, so can I, and so can you. This is the best way for me to get there unless something magical happens where I can go viral and my Instagram booms. But unfortunately, it hasn't happened yet, so the best way to get there little by little is by using my system. Other social media pays as well, but Instagram is my outlet, and I personally feel that it is easier to build followers on Instagram when using my system. And you don't have to post anything at all and can still build followers, whereas you must constantly post videos, tweets, or pictures on other social media platforms.

Instagram is also one of the most successful social media platforms out there, which is beneficial for me. A few ways to make money on Instagram are by selling merchandise, becoming an influencer and partnering with brands, opening an Instagram shop, offering Instagram marketing services, or even selling photos, illustrations, or digital files. There are a few more ways; all you have to do is find information and do more research on it because everyone has their own ways to make extra money.

# CHAPTER 6

## How to Avoid Getting Suspended from Instagram

**THERE IS NOTHING WORSE** than getting suspended from Instagram, which means you can't do anything on Instagram at all. You can't post, follow, or like when Instagram suspends your account. I've gotten suspended a couple of times, usually for about three to seven days. This has slowed my process in growing my followers, but now I've gotten smarter about avoiding it through trial and error.

Now I try to avoid getting suspended by following Instagram's guidelines. One way to get suspended is trying to follow too many people at one time can backfire. Like I stated before, try to add about one hundred people at a time; if you add too many, you will get suspended for a couple of days. Another way to get suspended for seven days is by unfollowing more than three hundred people in one day. So try not to unfollow 300; try 250, and wait another two days before you start unfollowing again.

If you post anything that goes against Instagram's guidelines, you can also get suspended. And if Instagram feels that what you posted violates its content guidelines, it will delete your Instagram, and you won't be able to get your account back.

# CHAPTER 7

## Why Putting Videos on Your Instagram Feed Is Better Than Posting Pictures

**I'VE NOTICED THAT THE** majority of people don't hit the Like button or comment on people's pictures or videos. I've followed thousands and thousands of people and seen many pictures with so few likes. I still don't understand why, but that is the way it is. They will view your picture and keep scrolling. Even your real friends will do that, and it happens all the time—unless you are a superstar, which I am not. Noticing this, I made a conscious decision to post only videos on my Instagram feed. Even if my followers don't hit the Like button, if they view my video, I am very happy. As one example of how people will view a video but not hit Like, on a birthday video from 2021, I have more than seventeen thousand views and only nine hundred likes.

# CHAPTER 8

## How to Get Certified Stars to Follow You Back

I USUALLY SET A day when all I do is concentrate on following certified accounts. I am not talking about superstars like Selena Gomez or Cristiano Ronaldo. I am talking about certified accounts like sports players, authors, and artists—pretty much anyone who has a certified check mark. But I do have a couple of certified followers who have millions of followers. To be honest, I got lucky, because it's extremely hard to get followed by them. But let's not talk about the certified stars who have millions of followers; let's concentrate on the ones who have only a few thousand followers. You're going to find out that not every certified account has a high number of followers. You have a better chance of getting followed by them; you just need to know how to do it.

First, your page needs to be eye-catching, and most importantly, you can't be following thousands of people. People will follow you only if they notice that you have thousands and thousands of followers and are not following many accounts. My suggestion is to have about ten to fifteen thousand followers and follow only one thousand people. This will catch users' attention, and some will follow you back. It's going to take some time, but one check mark at a time. If you do not have these numbers, the chances of a certified account following you back are very slim. I keep all of my certified followers, and I will never unfollow them. Having certified accounts following me back looks great, and for me it's an honor.

Another way I was able to get followed by them was writing them a note letting them know how I would love to connect with great influencers and that I would highly appreciate it if they followed me back. Sometimes it has worked, but many times it hasn't.

I have more than one hundred certified accounts following me back, and in time I will have more. You need to be patient because it is going to take some time; just work the system, and you will get there in due time. I also tried sending Dwayne "The Rock" Johnson a message, but he never responded. But that's OK; at least I tried.

# CHAPTER 9

# Be Careful with Scammers

**THERE ARE MANY SCAMMERS** out there, especially on Instagram. I get many people messaging me about investing, growing my Instagram numbers, and requesting that I help them out because they can't log into their Instagram account. They will try to send you a link; do not click on any link they send you because they may take over your account. Just ignore them because they are all scammers. People are out there trying to get your information and your money. People also want to take your Instagram account, and once they do, they will ask you to pay them to get your account back. It has happened to so many people; I even watched an episode of the news about it. Whoever asks you for any type of help or to make an investment, do not fall for their scam. Also there are people that claim they have won the lottery and looking for anyone that needs money do not fall for this either. And this advice goes to all men out there: if you get a female that wants to share explicit videos, DO NOT share anything with them, because they will record it and start blackmailing you by telling you if you don't pay them such-and-such amount, they will expose you to your family and friends. Be really smart because many men can get caught up in this scheme.

There are also people messaging you claiming they can help grow your Instagram numbers. Do not do it; be smart and just unfollow them or block them. One way to really secure your account and prevent hackers is to go to your settings and go to double identification; this way, you can protect your account. Don't respond to people messaging you and asking who you are; just make them wonder. You don't know them anyway, so it's OK. I have so many messages that I don't even read unless I know the person, and even then, I try not to answer many back. No need to; I refuse to get scammed.

# CHAPTER 10

## Is Instagram Appropriate for Children?

**ACCORDING TO THE TERMS** of service, you must be thirteen years of age to have an Instagram account. But there's no age verification process, so it's very easy for children under the age of thirteen to sign up. This is a huge problem. Anyone can open an Instagram account, and you wouldn't know who the person is because there are so many fake accounts out there. There are many stalkers and pedophiles who can use this social media platform for bad things. Kids are very vulnerable out there, and they can be easily manipulated by fake accounts. Kids can also follow certain profiles and hashtags that are not age appropriate and can easily be misleading. This is a huge problem, especially if parents are not monitoring their accounts. Just please monitor your kids with any social media out there.

**I WANT TO TAKE** the time and thank everyone who has read my book, from the bottom of my heart, I truly appreciate it. I really want to help people understand the pros and cons of Instagram. I hope this book can help readers build their Instagram numbers for themselves or new business adventure. It took me many years to develop this system and I hope it can help people as well. These are all my secrets and I decided to share it with the world.

**IF YOU HAVE ANY** questions, feel free to add my Instagram account @carlitoskyisthelimit. You can contact me, I'm here to help. I Hope to hear from you soon!